Low Calorie

Desserts and Snacks

Pat Cher

Dieting, some thoughts...

Basically, losing weight is calorie in calorie out.

http://familydoctor.org/online/famdocen/home/healthy/food/improve/795.printerview.html

Check on your ideal body weight at

http://www.halls.md/ideal-weight/body.htm

Some strategies...

For most people controlling food intake at breakfast and lunch is easier than later in the day. It can be routine.

For example if you're on a 1500 calorie diet, try having 200 calories for breakfast and the 300 for lunch. Make it a routine, but routine or not, it has to be something satisfying.

Here's an example... a 200 calorie breakfast pizza.

1 small pita (125 calories)

3 slices of tomato (free calories) chopped

Spread on the pita and add

1/4 cup of low fat cheddar cut in small pieces (57 Calories).

Put under the broiler until the cheese starts to bubble.

Keeping track of calories is important. You can do that in one of three ways;

-Track it on an App, there a quite a few of them you can download for free at the Apple Apps store.

-Write everything you eat down and include the calories.

-Plan menus ahead of time. For example, if you're on a 1500 calories diet, plan 200 calories for breakfast, 300 for lunch and 500 for dinner. The other 500 is for snacks or to supplement a meal when you're feeling extra hungry.

(Of course, you should check with your doctor before starting any diet program, especially if you have health problems)

Pumpkin Dessert Supreme

16 servings 95 calories each

4 c cooked pumpkin

3/4 c 1% milk

2 eggs

1 tsp. vanilla

3/4 c flour

1/4 c brown sugar

2 tsp. cinnamon

1 tsp. ginger

1/4 tsp. cloves (optional)

Topping

1/2 c flour

2 tbsp. brown sugar

2 tbsp. butter

Beat the eggs lightly. Add cooked pumpkin, milk, and vanilla. Mix

Add flour and brown sugar and spices. Mix. Pour into a greased 13 by 9 inch pan. Mix topping until crumbly and sprinkle on top.

Bake at 350 for 30 to 40 minutes or until a knife inserted in centre comes out clean.

Light Crepe Batter

(Light and scrumptious. Make larger than usual crepes for cakes (see below). Use 8 or 9 inches fry pan.) Makes 7 large 78 calories each

1 c flour

1 tsp. baking powder

4 egg whites

1 tbsp. icing sugar

1 c skim milk

1 tsp. vanilla

Mix dry ingredients. Beat egg whites and add other liquids. Gradually pour into flour mixture, beating to eliminate lumps. Cool in refrigerator for at least1 hour. Heat frying (8 or 9 in) pan until a drop of water poured on it sizzles. Take off the stove, spray with oil to coat. Pour batter with large spoon or with measuring cup. Spread, tipping batter until it covers the pan. Return pan to stove. Cook until bottom is brown and you see small bubbles popping up. Flip and brown the other side. Transfer to a plate.

Strawberry Crepe Cake Filling

38 calories per serving when each pie is divided into 8 servings 51 calories per serving if each pie is divided into 6 servings

1 pkg. Strawberry gelatin
1/2 c water
2 c frozen strawberries
1/2 c Cool Whip thawed

Place frozen strawberries, water and gelatin in saucepan, and slowly bring to a boil, stirring frequently. Reduce heat and simmer for 3 minutes.

Remove form heat and cool. Stir in thawed cool whip. Refrigerate until firm, about 3 hours.

Assembling the Cake

Place a crepe on the platter and add enough filling to spread to the edges of the crepe. Spread evenly. Continue using four of the crepes. Decorate the top layer with the filling, cool whip, and a few strawberries. Chill until firm and cut. Delicious and light!

Pistachio Crepe Cake

Serves 8, 67 calories each. Divide into 16, and it lowers the calories to 33 per serving.

This sounds like a lot of work but if you make the crepe batter in the morning, let it rest for an hour and cook later, it doesn't seem to take as much time. The cake assembly itself is done in less than five minutes.

Pistachio Filling

1 pkg. Pistachio instant pudding sugar free

1 c skim milk

3 tbsp. cool whip thawed

In a bowl, add milk to pudding mix, and stir until mixed. Fold in cool whip. Cool until it gets firm.

Assembling the Cake

Place a crepe on the platter and add enough filling to spread to the edges of the crepe. Spread evenly. Continue using four of the crepes. Decorate the top layer with the filling, cool whip, and maybe a few strawberries. Chill until firm and cut. Delicious and light!

Strawberry Crepes Filling

Serves 4, 50 calories each

2 c strawberries

1/4 c light sour cream

2 tsp. icing sugar

Chop strawberries. Keep a few for the top. Add half the sour cream to the strawberries and mix.

Place 1/2 cup strawberries mixture on each crepe. Roll. Place 1/2 tbsp. of sour cream on top of each crepe. Add a few strawberries for decoration. Sprinkle with 1/2 tsp. icing sugar.

Apple Crepes Filling

Serves 4, 60 calories each

2 apples

2 tsp. butter

2 tsp. sugar

Peel and slice apples.

Add butter to fry pan, and simmer the apples until they soften. Add sugar and cook for another minute. Remove from heat. Add cinnamon. Let cool slightly.

Place filling on the crepes, roll up and serve. A dollop of light cream on top makes a nice presentation. (1 tbsp. light whipped cream adds 4 to 7 calories)

Mixes

Want cakes already portioned for you like the ones sold by Weight Watchers? Why not make your own from a mix?

Use small loaf pans, I use Baker's Secret 8 loaf pan, similar to muffin pans (you could also use muffin pans).

Divide the mix into 2 of those loaf pans. Makes 16 cakes in all which are bigger then the Weight Watcher ones.

The Baker's Secret pans make loaves that are bigger than individual servings so I cut them in half, and make frosting with icing sugar a dab of butter and vanilla. I add water to make the icing very loose. Spread on the cakes, the icing with seep in. Yummy.

Diet tip: Put these in the freezer and take out as needed. They thaw quickly and are delicious cold. Also, if they're in the freezer, you tend to forget them until you really need the sugar fix.

Easy Spice Cake

74 calories per serving for 32 mini cake halves or 24 muffins at 99 calories each

1 pkg. spice cake mix

1 c canned plain pumpkin

4 egg whites

1 c water

Combine all ingredients and mix well. Spray pans with cooking spray.

Divide mixture into 2 mini loaf pans or two muffin pans.

Bake in preheated 350 degree oven until cake begins to brown and a toothpick inserted in centre comes out clean, about 25 minutes.

Yellow Cake

72 calories per serving for 32 mini cake halves or 24 muffins at 97 calories each

1 pkg. yellow (or substitute other flavor) cake mix

1/3 c unsweetened applesauce

1 1/4 c water

3 egg whites

Combine all ingredients and mix well. spray pans with cooking spray.

Divide mixture into 2 mini loaf pans or two muffin pans.

Bake in preheated 350 degree oven until cake begins to brown and a toothpick inserted in centre comes out clean, about 25 minutes.

Quick Cake

Serves 12, 100 calories per serving

1 angel food cake

2 Vanilla or chocolate Sugar Free Pudding

3/4 c COOL WHIP

6 strawberries

Cut cake into two layers. Place bottom layer, on plate and spread with chocolate pudding. Cover with other layer. Spread top with Cool Whip. Decorate with strawberries.

Vanilla Wafer Cookies

Makes 16, 45 calories each or makes 20, 36 calories each. Awesome by themselves or great for ice cream sandwiches, or icebox cake, and so easy to make!

3 tbsp. butter

2 egg whites

5 tbsp. flour

1/2 c icing sugar

A few drops vanilla extract

Place butter in mixing dish (I used medium size). Melt butter in microwave. Pour the rest of the ingredients over the melted butter.

Whisk until smooth. Use cookie sheet lined with parchment paper. Drop two teaspoons at a time.

Cookies should be at least 2 inches apart. A cookie sheet should hold no more than nine cookies. They spread a lot. (If you don't have parchment paper use foil which has been heavily sprayed with oil.) This recipe makes 16 to 20 wafers.

Peanut Butter Cookies

Makes 36 cookies 41 calories each, 51 calories if using regular peanut butter.

1/3 c margarine

1/2 c light peanut butter

1/4 cp brown sugar

1 egg

1 tsp. vanilla

1/2 c bran

1/2 c flour

1 tsp. baking soda

Cream margarine, peanut butter, sugar, eggs and vanilla. Add flour, bran and baking soda. Blend.

Mix well. Form mixture into 1 inch round balls, and place on greased cookie sheet. Flatten with fork. Bake at 350 until golden brown, about 10 minutes.

Mini Peanut Butter Cookies

Makes 18 mini cookies 75 calories each

1/4 c flour

1/4 tsp. baking powder

1 c light peanut butter

1/4 c applesauce unsweetened

 2 egg whites

Mix peanut butter, applesauce and egg whites, add flour and baking powder.

Drop on greased cookie sheets or mini muffin cups.Use about 2 teaspoons per cookie.

Bake at 350 degrees for 10 to 12 minutes, or until cookies begin to brown.

Makes about 18 mini cookies.

Date Macaroons

58 calories per serving for 12 large or 29 calories for 24 mini macaroons

1/2 c dates cut in small pieces

1tbsp flour

2 egg whites (room temperature)

1/4 tsp. cream of tartar

1/4 tsp. salt

1 tsp. vanilla

1/2 c sugar

Coat dates with flour. Beat egg white and cream of tartar until soft peaks form. Keep beating while adding salt and vanilla. Continue beating, adding sugar gradually. Stop processing, and fold in the dates. Use teaspoon to place on greased baking sheet.

Bake at 350 degrees until cookies begin to brown, twelve to fifteen minutes.

Puffed Wheat Balls

65 calories per serving for 24 large balls or 32 calories for 48 mini balls

1/2 c corn syrup

3 tbsp. butter

3 tsp. cocoa (optional)

1/2 c sugar

8 c puffed wheat

Place first 4 ingredients in saucepan. Bring to a boil. Let it bubble for 2 minutes while stirring.

Remove from heat and pour over puffed wheat. Stir until cereal is well covered. When cool enough to handle make into balls. You may need to add a little cooking spray on your hands to make it easier to handle.

Let cool until firm.

Puffed Wheat Crackle

53 calories per serving for 24 large balls, or 27 calories for 48 mini balls

1/2 c molasses

1 c sugar

1/3 c water

11/2 tsp. vinegar

2 tsp. butter

2 tsp. vanilla

8 c puffed wheat.

Place puffed wheat in large buttered dish. Place other ingredients except butter in saucepan and boil until the syrup shows brittle when placed into a cup of cold water.

Add butter and stir. Pour over the puffed wheat, and stir until well coated. Press down to even out. Cut into squares.

Ladyfinger Cookies

(A quick fix)

62 calories per cookie

12 Ladyfingers

4 tbsp. sugar free Strawberry jam

4 tbsp. Chocolate syrup

Split Ladyfingers in half lengthwise. Spread with 1/2 tsp strawberry jam. Drizzle each with 1/2 tsp chocolate syrup.

Crispy Sweet Ball

Makes 18, 31 calories each

1 tbsp. butter

1/2 c chopped dates

¼ cup sugar

1 1/2 c Rice Krispies

In large saucepan, on medium heat, melt butter. Add dates and sugar Cook until thickened.

Let cool until easy to handle. Add cereal to saucepan and mix. Coat hands with oil or cooking spray and divide mixture to make 18 balls. Cool and eat. Store in fridge.

Popcorn Squares

Makes 48 squares, 28 calories each

12 c popped corn

3/4 c brown sugar

1/4 c margarine

3 tbsp. corn syrup

1/4 tsp. baking soda

1/2 tsp. vanilla

Arrange popped corn on cookie sheet. Pour the brown sugar, margarine and corn syrup in saucepan and simmer for 3 minutes. Mixture should be bubbling gently. Remove from heat and add baking soda and vanilla and stir.

Pour over the popped corn and mix well. Pat into the pan.

Bake at 400 for 10 minutes. Cut while still warm or break into pieces when cooled.

Light Apple Crisp

53 calories for 6 servings

3 apples

1/4 tsp. brown sugar

1/4 c rolled oats

1/4 c Cool Whip Light

Pare apples and slice, place in microwave dish which has been sprayed with cooking spray. Mix oats and brown sugar. Pour over apples, sprinkle with water to moisten.

Cover with saran and microwave for 1 minute. Let cool and divide into six.

Carrot Bar

16 bars, 81 calories per serving

1c flour

1tsp baking powder

1tsp cinnamon

1/8 tsp. nutmeg

2 tbsp. sugar

1 tbsp. butter

1/2 c hot water

3 egg whites

2 c carrots

1 c raisin

Combine dry ingredients. Stir in egg whites. Add carrots and raisins. Mix well. add butter to hot water, stir until butter is melted. Add to batter. Mix.

Pour into greased 9 inch square pan. Bake for 35 minutes at 350 or until inserted toothpick comes out clean.

Cool and cut into 2 inch squares.

Chocolate Squares

Makes 24, 53 calories each

2 c graham cracker crumbs

1 c skim milk

1/2 c semi-sweet chocolate

1 tsp. vanilla

2 tsp. icing sugar

Combine graham crackers and milk. Mix until mushy. Melt chocolate and add to mixture along with vanilla. Mix well.

Pat into greased 9 inch pan. Bake at 350 degrees for 15 minutes or until firm. Cool, sprinkle with icing sugar and cut into 24 pieces.

Graham Cracker Crust

Serves 8 at 65 calories per portion

1 1/4 c graham wafer crumbs

3 tbsp. low sugar strawberry jam

Mix ingredients together. Place in greased pie pan and press to even out the crust along sides and bottom.

Bake at 350 until firm, about 10 minutes. Note: This is a bit mushy to handle but tastes delicious. The mixture will be moist and likely to stick unless you spray your hands with cooking spray.

Meringue Crust

67 calories per serving when cut into 8 pieces 89 calories per serving when cut into 6 pieces

2 egg whites

1/4 tsp. cream of tartar

1/4 tsp. salt

1/2 tsp. vanilla

1/2 c white sugar

Make sure egg whites are at room temperature. Place egg whites in clean dry bowl. Beat, adding cream of tartar and salt. Continue beating until soft peaks form. Add vanilla and then the sugar, a tablespoon at a time.

Beat until stiff. Mixture should look glossy and be stiff all the way through. Place in greased pie pans.(You may also use baking sheet. Make large circle with mixture and push edges up slightly.)

Bake in 400 degree oven for about 45-50 minutes. Cool before adding filling.

Rice Crisp Crust

82 calories for 1/8 of pie

4 tsp. peanut butter

1 tbsp. honey

2 c Rice Krispie cereal

Melt peanut butter and honey in microwave. Place cereal in large bowl and add peanut butter and honey.

Mix well. Press mixture in pie plate or pan and refrigerate. Add filling when crust has cooled.

Corn Flakes Pie Crust

76 calories for 1/8 of pie

1 c Corn Flakes

2 tbsp. sugar

1/4 c margarine

Melt sugar and margarine in microwave. Place cereal in a large bowl. Add sugar and margarine mixture Mix well.

Press mixture in pie plate or pan and refrigerate. Add filling when crust has cooled.

Sweet Potato Crust

72 calories per serving when cut into 8 pieces 97 calories per serving when cut into 6 pieces

2 c sweet potatoes, peeled and grated (use food processor)

1 tsp. salt

2 1/2 tbsp. all-purpose flour

1/4 tsp. cinnamon

1 tbsp. oil

Preheat oven to 375 degrees. Combine sweet potatoes and salt, and place in colander. Drain for 20 minutes. Press to remove excess liquid. Place in bowl and add flour, 3/4 tbsp. of the oil and cinnamon. Mix well.

Place mixture in greased pie plate and press to form crust. Brush with remaining 1/4 tbsp. oil (use basting brush).

Bake the crust until it begins to brown, 25 to 30 minutes.

Peanut Butter Mousse or Pie Filling

8 servings 75 calories each 6 servings, 99 calories each

1 tbsp. Peanut Butter

1 tbsp. sugar

2 c cool whip

Mix peanut butter and sugar then fold in cool whip. Voila, it's done!

Strawberry Mousse or Filling

38 calories per serving when each pie is divided into 8 servings, 51 calories per serving when each pie is divided into 6 servings

1 pkg. Strawberry gelatin
1/2 c water
2 c frozen strawberries
1/2 c cool whip thawed

Place frozen strawberries, water and gelatin in saucepan, and slowly bring to a boil, stirring frequently.

Reduce heat and simmer for 3 minutes.

Remove form heat and cool.
Stir in thawed cool whip.
Pour on pie shell or for mousse pour in a bowl.
Refrigerate until firm, about 3 hours.

Strawberry Mousse or Filling 2

Serves 4, 92 calories each

3 c strawberries, sliced (Keep a few for garnish.)

1/2 c water

1/4 c sugar

1 tbsp. cornstarch

In saucepan, add 1 cup of strawberries and half the water, bring to a boil, and then simmer for 3 minutes, stirring frequently.

In bowl add rest of water, cornstarch and sugar and stir to mix. Add cornstarch mixture to strawberry mixture in saucepan. Bring to a boil.

Stir until sauce thickens.

Cool slightly.

Place the rest of the strawberries in bottom of pie shell.

Top the strawberries with the sauce.

Refrigerate until cool.

Top with cool whip and remaining strawberries.

Strawberry Mousse or Filling 3

65 calories for 8 servings 86 calories for 6 servings

1 c of Vanilla instant pudding sugar free

1 c 1% milk

1 c cool whip thawed

3 c strawberries, sliced

In a bowl, add milk to pudding mix, and stir until mixed.

Add 1 cup of strawberries.

Mix loosely

Fold in cool whip.

Layer mixture and remaining strawberries in piecrust or dessert bowl.

Cool until firm.

Key Lime Pie Filling or Mousse

For 6 servings size 94 calories each For 8 servings size 70 calories each

1 pkg. fat-free key lime yoghurt

1 container fat free frozen whipped topping

1/4 c water

1 pkg. lime gelatin sugar free

Heat water to boiling, add gelatin.

Stir until dissolved.

Add yoghurt and mix well.

Fold in frozen whipped topping.

Pour in piecrust or dessert dish.

Refrigerate until set, 3 to 4 hours.

Carrot Pudding or Pie Filling

Serves 8, 70 calories each

2 c carrots

3 egg whites

1 c 1% milk

1/2 c brown sugar

1 tsp. cinnamon 1tsp nutmeg

1/2 tsp. ginger

Place egg whites, milk sugar and spices in food processor. Mix well.

Cook carrots until tender.

Cool and add to food processor mixture. Process until smooth.

Pour on pie shell or in oven proof serving dish.

Bake in 425 degree oven for 10 minutes.

Reduce heat to 350 and bake for 30 to 35 minutes longer or until toothpick inserted in center comes out clean.

Frozen Chocolate Cream Treats

Makes 6 servings

70 calories per serving when using instant pudding mix with sugar, 23 calories each with sugar free pudding mix

1 pkg. Chocolate Instant Pudding mix
2 c 1% milk

Add milk to Chocolate Instant Pudding
Mix well.
Pour into popsicle molds or paper cups.
Freeze.
Insert wooden stick when the popsicles are almost done.

Apple Ginger Smoothie

Serves 2, 57 calories each

1/4 apple

1/2 c pineapple

1/8 tsp. ginger

1/2 c apple juice

1 1/4 c ice cubes

Process the fruit in processor until mushy.

Add ice cubes.

Process.

Add apple juice.

Process.

Serve right away.

Banana Ice

Serves 2, 98 calories each

1 ripe banana

1 tbsp. sugar

1/2 c skim milk

3 c ice cubes

Process first 3 ingredients in blender at high speed.

Add ice a cup at a time and process until creamy.

You may not need 3 cups of ice, blend only until creamy.

Do not over process, or it will get mushy.

Serve right away.

Peanut Butter and Banana Frozen Candies

Makes 8 pieces, 23 calories each

1 banana (ripe is better)

1 tbsp. light peanut butter

Cut Banana in half lengthwise.

Spread peanut butter on one banana half like you would a sandwich.

Put banana back together.

Slice banana into 8 equal pieces.

Place bananas on wax paper covered plate.

Freeze.

When frozen, place in freezer safe bags.

Banana Logs

Makes 4 servings 73 calories each

2 bananas

2 tbsp. chocolate syrup light

1/4 c Rice Krispies

Cup Bananas in half crosswise.

Insert stick into end of each banana piece.

Roll banana in chocolate sauce, then in cereal.

Place on tray lined with waxed paper and freeze.

Quick Frozen Treats

Freeze the following fruit in plastic baggies or containers. Take out when you need a quick sweet fix.

Grapes

Honey dew melon (cut in small pieces or use melon baller)

Fat free yogurt in small containers

Pineapple cut in small pieces

Peach slices

Sliced banana

Strawberry Mint Pops

Serves 6, 60 calories each

1/4 c mints

1 pkg. strawberry jell-o

1 pkg. unsweetened strawberry drink mix

2 cups water

Bring 1 c of water to a boil.

Add mints.

Stir until mints dissolve.

Add gelatin.

Mix well.

Add 1 c ice water, and stir well.

Pour in cups or molds.

Freeze.

Add stick when almost frozen solid.

Strawberry Cream Pops

Serves 6, 55 calories each

2 cups fresh or frozen strawberries.

1 c plain sugar free yoghurt

1/4 c sugar

Place the strawberries in blender or food processor.

This works better if strawberries are sliced or chopped.

Process until pureed.

Add yoghurt and sugar.

Blend. Pour in cups or mold.

Freeze.

Add stick when almost frozen solid.

Watermelon Pops

Serves 6, 15 calories each

2 cups watermelon, seeds removed

Cube watermelon and place in blender.

Blend until smooth.

Pour in cups or molds.

Freeze.

Add stick when almost frozen solid.

Chocolate Popsicles

Serves 6, 40 calories each

1 pkg. sugar free chocolate instant pudding

2 1/2 c skim milk

Mix instant pudding and milk.

Pour in cups or mold.

Freeze.

Add stick when almost frozen solid.

Orange Pops

Makes 6 servings 72 calories per serving (gelatin with sugar) 23 calories per serving with sugar free gelatin.

1 pkg. orange flovoured gelatin

1 cup boiling water

1 cup orange juice

Stir gelatin in boiling water until dissolved.

Add orange juice.

Mix well.

Pour into pop molds or paper cups.

Freeze.

Insert wooden stick when the pops are almost done.

Strawberry Yummy

Serves 4, 65 calories each

2 cups fresh or frozen strawberries

1 pkg. vanilla pudding mix(sugar free and the kind you cook)

1 pkg. sugar-free strawberry flavored gelatin

2 c water

Clean strawberries and slice.

Arrange at bottom of deep dish.

In cooking pot, combine pudding mix, strawberry gelatin, and water.

Bring to a boil, stirring frequently.

Let boil for at least a minute while stirring.

Pour over strawberries.

Refrigerate until cooled and solid.

Top with cool whip or light whipping cream.

Fruit Cobbler

Serves 4, 59 calories each

1 medium apple

3/4 c strawberries

2 ladyfingers

1/4 c cool whip lite

Pare apples and slice.

Microwave for 30 seconds or until they soften.

Microwave 1/4 c strawberries on medium for 30 seconds or until they become runny.

Divide ingredients into 4 and place in small glass (shrimp cocktail size glasses), alternating the layers.

Top with cool whip lite.

Place half a ladyfinger in the glass.

Quick Berry Jell-o

Serves 4, 12 calories each

1 pkg. jelly powder light (any flavor)

1 cup boiling water

7 ice cubes (3/4 c) It doesn't have to be exact.

1/4 cup frozen berries (I used strawberries)

1 tbsp. whipped topping

Put powder in blender, and pour the hot water through as the blender runs on whip.

Add ice cubes in one at a time, waiting a few seconds between each.

Let the mixture whip for about a minute.

Place the frozen berries in individual cups or in an 8 by 9 glass pan.

Pour mixture over the berries.

Place in fridge.

Ready in 15 minutes.

Enjoy.

Apple Strawberry Dessert

Serves 4, 79 calories each

2 apple pared and sliced

1 c strawberries

2 tbsp. brown sugar

2 tbsp. flour

1/2 tsp. cinnamon optional

Mix fruit together with sugar and flour until fruit is well coated.

Place in greased baking dish. (I like this in a glass ovenproof dish).

Bake at 400 degrees for 20 to 25 minutes or until apples are tender.

Serve warm with thawed frozen whipped topping or cool and serve in parfait glasses intermingled with dollops of frozen whipped topping

Strawberries Dipped in Chocolate

One of our family favorites Serves 4, 83 calories each

2 cups Strawberries

11/2 squares semi sweet chocolate

Place chocolate squares in microwave safe serving dish, and melt chocolate squares in microwave.

Remove every 20 to 30 seconds and mix.

When chocolate is smooth and without lumps, serve with strawberries.

If you don't like people dipping into the same bowl, provide spoons so the chocolate can be placed on individual plates.

Fruit Dipped in Chocolate

Serves 4, 100 calories each (if shared equally)

1/2 square semi sweet chocolate 80 calories

1 medium apple 95 calories

1 orange 62 calories

1 c pineapple chunks 82 calories

1 c sliced pear 81 calories

Place chocolate squares in microwave-safe serving dish, and melt, removing every 20 to 30 seconds to mix.

Place fruit on serving tray along with toothpicks.

Place the bowl with the chocolate in middle of the fruit plate.

Dip fruit in chocolate and enjoy.

Lemon Dip

Serves 12, 19 calories each

Good with fruit or raw vegetables.

1 cup lemon or plain yoghurt

2/12 tbsp. icing sugar

1 tsp. lemon juice

Mix and enjoy! Place on fruit tray with lemon wedges. Yummy!

Irish Cream Fruit Dip

Serves 12, 50 calories each

1 c light sour cream

1 tbsp. brown sugar

1 tbsp. Irish Cream liqueur or omit and add a tsp vanilla

Use with your favorite fruit; apples slices, orange sections, bananas, strawberries, kiwi wedges, pear slices... Enjoy!

Quick Fruit Dip

Serves 12. 45 calories each

1 c light sour cream

1 tbsp. sugar free, fat free, vanilla pudding mix

(Use the dry mix. save the rest for when you make your next dip or add by spoonful to other desserts to enhance flavor.

Mix two ingredients together and serve.

Poppy Seed Dip

Serves 12, 25 calories each

1 c low fat vanilla yoghurt

1 tbsp. honey

3 tsp. lemon juice

2 tsp. poppy seeds

Mix everything together. Use with salad or use as dip with vegetables or fruit.

Apple with Creamy Stuffing

Serves 2, 65 calories each

1 apple, cut in half and cored

2 tbsp. fat free cottage cheese

1 tbsp. fat free cream cheese

1/2 tsp. vanilla

Mix cottage cheese, cream cheese and vanilla. Place on cored apple halves. Serve.

Strawberry or Fruit Leather

24 pieces, 10 calories each

2 cups strawberry or fruit puree (made in blender or food processor)

1 tbsp. lemon juice

1 tbsp. corn syrup

Mix all three ingredients until well blended. Pour onto well greased jellyroll pan leaving an inch all around.

Mixture should be spread thin. Place in 180 degree oven and let dry for 7 to 8 hours. Cut into strips while still warm. Place strips on waxed paper or saran and store in plastic containers.

Spicy Watermelon

Serves 12, 5 calories each

1 c diced watermelon

1 c lime juice

A few drops of hot sauce (to taste)

Pour lime juice in small bowl. Add hot pepper sauce and mix. Arrange watermelon pieces on platter, and have toothpicks available for serving. Place lime dip in center.

Pear and Apple Chips

Pears 1 pear 81 calories Apples 1 apple 72 calories

Use as many or as little of the fruit as you want. I like to make a lot because the oven is on for quite a while. Make these when the oven is going to be on for other baking.

Slice apples width wise for a more pleasing shape. Pear can be cut either way. Slices should not be extra thin, about 1/8 inch.

Thicker slices will take longer to bake.

Place slices on sprayed cookie sheet, and bake until the slices are dry (60 to 90 minutes) at 200 degrees.

Turn slices a few times during baking.

Cool. Give the slices a bit of a twist while still warm to make them look like regular chips (optional).

Sprinkle with salt or sugar while still warm.

Apple Syrup

Serves 8 (1 tbsp.) 27 calories each

1 c unsweetened apple juice

2 tbsp. brown sugar

1 tbsp. cornstarch

1/2 tsp. vanilla

Place all the ingredients in a saucepan except vanilla, mix, and bring to a boil. Simmer for 3 minutes stirring occasionally. Remove mixture from stove, and then add the vanilla and stir.

Strawberry Buttermilk Soup

88 calories per serving, makes 8 servings

2 c strawberries

1/4 c orange juice

1/2 c sugar

1/12 c water

2 c buttermilk

Combine all ingredients in saucepan except buttermilk. Bring to a boil.

Simmer for 20 minutes. Remove from heat.

If you like a smooth soup, you may remove the berries and put them through the food processor.

Add buttermilk.

Chill for at least two hours.

Serve.

Garnish with orange slices or berries.

Raspberry Soup

100 calories per 3/4 cup serving

2 c raspberries fresh or frozen

1/2 cup sugar 2 cup water 2 lemons

1 stick cinnamon

2 cup yogurt plain

Combine all ingredients in saucepan except yogurt.

Bring to a boil.

Remove from heat.

Remove lemon slices and cinnamon stick.

If you like a smooth soup, you may remove the berries and put them through the food processor.

Chill for at least two hours.

Serve.

Garnish with lemon slices or berries.

Mixed Fruit Soup

Serves 4, 75 calories per cup.

2 cup canned or bottled sour cherries

1 c peaches

1/2 c orange juice

1/2 c cranberry juice

1 stick cinnamon

1 tsp. sugar

Reserve cherries.

Place liquid from cherries with juice, cinnamon and sugar in pot.

Simmer on medium heat for 5 minutes.

Remove cinnamon stick.

Add cherries and thinly sliced peaches.

Cool until chilled, about 2 hours.

Serve.

Pineapple Peach Soup

Serves 12, 90 calories each

4 c peaches

1 c pineapple

1 c orange juice

1 c pineapple juice

2 tsp. lemon juice

2 cplain low fat yogurt

Lemon or lime wedges

Peel peaches, slice and puree in food processor.

Pour in separate container

Puree the pineapple in a food processor, add to peaches.

Add to container.

Add the juices and yogurt, and mix well.

At this point soup may be strained for a finer texture.

Chill.

Pour in individual bowls and serve garnished with lemon or lime slices.

Cookie Popcorn

48 calories per cup

12 c popped corn

1 tbsp. butter

2 tbsp. sugar

1/4 tsp. nutmeg

1/2 tsp. cinnamon

Mix dry ingredients.

Add to popped corn.

Melt butter.

Add to popped corn and toss.

Enjoy!

Sweet Popcorn

61 calories per cup

12 cups popped corn

1 tbsp. butter

1/4 c honey

Arrange popped corn on greased cookie sheet.

Melt butter, and honey

Add to popped corn.

Toss to mix.

Bake at 300 degrees for 20 minutes, stirring once or twice. Cool and enjoy.

Peanut Butter Popcorn

84 calories per cup

12 cups popped corn

2 tbsp. butter

1/3 c light peanut butter

Mix butter and peanut butter and melt.

(If using microwave, cover the dish when melting butter and peanut butter). Add to popped corn and toss.

Creamy Mints

Makes 150 mints 18 Calories each

4 oz. Cream Cheese

3 1/2 c Icing Sugar (confectioner's)

A few drops peppermint flavoring (add more or less according to taste)

Food coloring optional

Cream cheese and icing sugar and peppermint flavor until well mixed. (At this point you may want to add food coloring.)

Cool in fridge for about an hour.

Roll into small balls (the size of a marble).

Place on waxed paper.

Press down with a fork.

Let it dry, and then place in airtight containers.

Store in fridge.

Creamy Maple Candies

(Tastes like Fudge) Use same recipe as Creamy Mints, but substitute Maple flavoring for peppermint.

Fudge

32 pieces, 20 calories each

1 c milk

3/4 c cocoa

3 tbsp. sugar

1 c water

1 tsp. vanilla

5 pkg. gelatin

Combine milk, sugar and cocoa in saucepan.

Simmer for 5 minutes stirring constantly. Mixture should start to thicken.

Pour water in another pan, add gelatin, and heat and stir to dissolve.

Add cocoa and milk mixture and vanilla to gelatin.

Stir until well mixed, and remove from heat.

Pour into 8 inch square pan.

Cool at room temperature until firm.

Cut into squares.

www.ingramcontent.com/pod-product-compliance
Lightning Source LLC
Chambersburg PA
CBHW080527030426
42337CB00023B/4656